Ready to Read

BASED ON **TIMOTHY GOES TO SCHOOL** AND OTHER STORIES BY

ROSEMARY WELLS

ILLUSTRATED BY MICHAEL KOELSCH

PUFFIN BOOKS

Hilltop School

DORIS

NORA

CLAUDE

FRANK

FRANK

"GOOD MORNING," says Mrs. Jenkins.
"Today we're going to learn an alphabet rhyme.
Who knows the alphabet?"
Timothy raises his hand. "I do!" he says.
"Wonderful," says Mrs. Jenkins. "You can help lead
the class in the rhyme."

The Next Step

What is the first letter of your name? How many words can you think of that start with that letter?

4

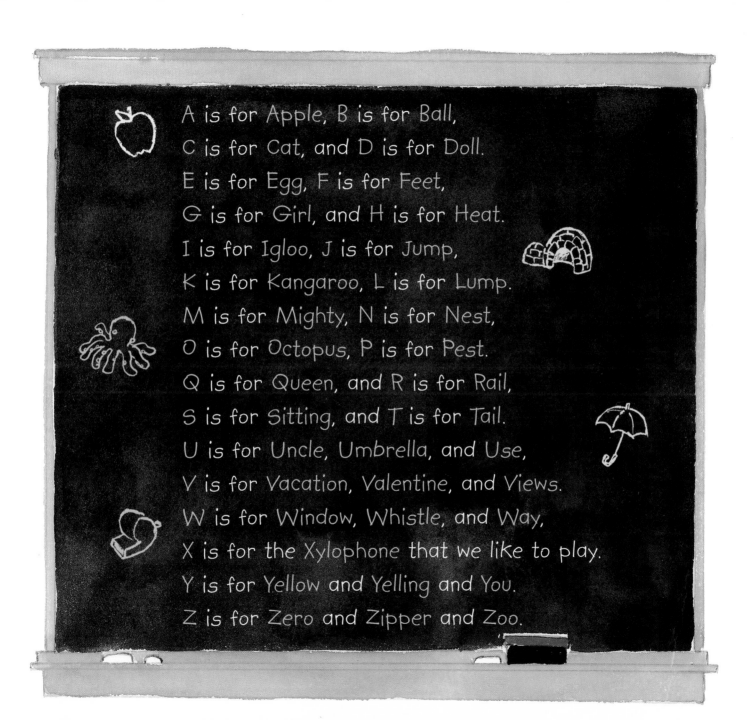

A is for Apple, B is for Ball,
C is for Cat, and D is for Doll.
E is for Egg, F is for Feet,
G is for Girl, and H is for Heat.
I is for Igloo, J is for Jump,
K is for Kangaroo, L is for Lump.
M is for Mighty, N is for Nest,
O is for Octopus, P is for Pest.
Q is for Queen, and R is for Rail,
S is for Sitting, and T is for Tail.
U is for Uncle, Umbrella, and Use,
V is for Vacation, Valentine, and Views.
W is for Window, Whistle, and Way,
X is for the Xylophone that we like to play.
Y is for Yellow and Yelling and You.
Z is for Zero and Zipper and Zoo.

"Now we're going to play a game," says Mrs. Jenkins. "Look at these three pictures. Two of the things pictured start with the same sound and one of them doesn't. Which one doesn't belong?"

"I get it," says Claude. "There's a picture of a ball, a picture of a car, and a picture of a book. BALL and BOOK both start with the B sound, but CAR starts with the C sound. So the car doesn't belong."

"Excellent," says Mrs. Jenkins. "Now try these sets of pictures." Look at the sets of pictures on the next page. Two things in each set start with the same sound, and one thing starts with a different sound. Which thing in each set doesn't belong?

The Next Step

Make your own picture sets of words that start with the same sound. Ask an adult to help you cut pictures from magazines to use in your sets.

6

1 2 3 4

"Who here is a good listener?" asks Mrs. Jenkins. Everybody raises their hands.

"Great!" says Mrs. Jenkins. "Then this should be easy. I want you all to listen carefully and tell me which word I need to complete the following sentence:

"To get to school, we ride the _____."

"I know!" says Timothy. "The missing word is BUS."

"Good," says Mrs. Jenkins. "Here's another sentence.

My favorite _____ is red. What word is missing?"

"Color!" says Nora. "The missing word is COLOR."

"Terrific," says Mrs. Jenkins. "You are all very good listeners."

 **The Next Step**

Make up your own sentence with a missing word. See if someone can guess the word that is missing.

8

Here are some sentences with missing words. Can you figure out which word is missing from each sentence?

Before she goes to school, Doris eats cereal for _____.

Timothy _____ when Yoko tells him a funny joke.

At recess, Nora likes to _____ hopscotch.

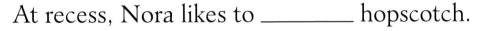

Charles is very sleepy. He is ready to go to _____.

At story time, Mrs. Jenkins reads *The Three Little Pigs* to the class.

When she's done reading, Mrs. Jenkins asks, "Who can tell me what happened?"

"One little pig built a house out of straw," says Yoko. "And one little pig built a house out of sticks."

"The other little pig built a house out of bricks," says Charles.

"The wolf blows down the straw house and the stick house," says Fritz,

"and all three pigs go hide in the brick house."

"The wolf tries to blow the brick house down, too," says Nora. "But he can't.

So he tries to get in through the chimney, but he falls into a pot of hot water."

"Then he runs away and the three little pigs live happily ever after," say the Franks.

"Perfect," says Mrs. Jenkins. "Now look at these four pictures about the story.

Can you put the pictures in the correct order?"

Can *you*? Look at the pictures on the next page and say what order they should go in.

The Next Step

What do you think happens to the three little pigs after the wolf runs away? Tell what you think might happen next in the story of *The Three Little Pigs*.

Today Officer Friendly is visiting Mrs. Jenkins's class to talk about safety.

"Road signs are very important," says Officer Friendly. "When you ride your bike or take a walk, road signs tell you what you need to know to stay safe. Who knows what this sign means?"

"It means *stop*!" says Fritz.

"Good," says Officer Friendly.

"What about this sign?"

"That means *don't walk*," says Yoko. "Cars might be coming and it is not safe to cross the street."

"Exactly," says Officer Friendly. "What a smart class you have, Mrs. Jenkins!" Look at the signs on the next page. Can you tell what each sign means by its picture, shape, or color? Can you read any words on the signs?

The Next Step

Take a walk through your neighborhood and look for road signs. How many do you see? Do you know what each sign means?

"Now we're going to build words," Mrs. Jenkins tells the class.

"Hooray!" say the Franks. "We love to build things."

"Then you'll be good word builders," says Mrs. Jenkins. "Let's start with the word ending AN. Who can build a word by adding a letter to the beginning of AN?"

"I can," says Timothy. "If you add a P to the beginning of AN, you get PAN."

"I know one!" says Nora. "If you add an F to the beginning of AN, you get FAN."

"And if you add an R to the beginning of AN, you get RAN," says Yoko.

How many words can you build using the word beginnings and endings below?

BEGINNINGS:	B	F	M	R	S	D
ENDINGS:	AT			IG		

The Next Step

Now try to build words by adding letters to the beginning of these word endings: OT   ING   AD
How many words can you build?

"I have a riddle," Claude says at recess. "I'm thinking of something you eat on your birthday that rhymes with RAKE."

"Is it CAKE?" asks Doris.

"That's it," says Claude. "CAKE rhymes with RAKE. Now it's your turn."

"Okay," says Doris. "I'm thinking of something you write with that rhymes with MEN."

"That's easy," say the Franks. "It's PEN. PEN rhymes with MEN. Now we have one. We're thinking of a color that rhymes with CLUE."

Can you solve the Franks' riddle?

See if you can answer these riddles, too:

What's an animal that says "meow" and rhymes with BAT?

What's something you drink from that rhymes with PUP?

What's something you ride in that rhymes with FAR?

 The Next Step
Make up your own rhyming riddle. Can anyone guess the answer?

"Every letter has two forms," says Mrs. Jenkins, "uppercase and lowercase. Uppercase letters look **LIKE THIS**. Lowercase letters look **like this**. Look at the letters I've written on the chalkboard. Who can match an uppercase letter with the same letter in lowercase?"

"I can," says Timothy. He matches the uppercase **T** with the lowercase **t**.

"Very good," says Mrs. Jenkins. "Who wants to be next?"

"I do," says Charles. He matches the uppercase **Y** with the lowercase **y**.

"Wonderful!" says Mrs. Jenkins. "Now let's do the rest."

Look at the letters on the chalkboard. Try to match each uppercase letter with the same letter in lowercase.

T	Y	M	A	E
e	m	t	a	y

The Next Step

Try to write your name using uppercase and lowercase letters. The first letter in your name should be in uppercase, and the rest of the letters should be in lowercase. Can you write your first name and your last name this way?

At music time, Timothy and his classmates sing "Old MacDonald Had a Farm."

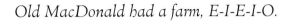

Old MacDonald had a farm, E-I-E-I-O.

*And on that farm he had a **cow**, E-I-E-I-O.*

*With a **moo moo** here and a **moo moo** there,*

*Here a **moo**, there a **moo**, everywhere a **moo moo**,*

Old MacDonald had a farm, E-I-E-I-O.

(For other verses, use dog/woof; pig/oink;
horse/neigh; rooster/cock-a-doodle-do; hen/cluck.)

"Good singing!" says Mrs. Jenkins. "Now who can tell
me the letters that begin the names of the animals?"
"I know," says Charles. "COW starts with the letter C."
"Correct," says Mrs. Jenkins. "What about PIG?"
Do you know the first letter in the word PIG?
Look at the pictures on this page and say the
letter that begins the name of each animal.

The Next Step

Name some other animals that are not pictured on this page.
What is the first letter in each animal name that you think of?

19

Mrs. Jenkins gives everyone a card with a picture on it. "Today we're going to play Rhyming Partners," she tells the class. "See if you can find a partner who has a picture of something that rhymes with the object on your card." Mrs. Jenkins helps everybody read the words on their cards. The word on Timothy's card is KING. He looks around for his rhyming partner. It's not Charles. He has a picture of a CAR. KING and CAR don't rhyme. It's not Nora. She has a picture of a MUG. MUG and KING don't rhyme.

It's Yoko! Her picture is of a RING. KING and RING rhyme. "You're my rhyming partner, Yoko!" says Timothy. Look at the cards on the next page and try to match up the rest of the rhyming partners in Mrs. Jenkins's class.

The Next Step

What are some words that rhyme with . . . SKATE   POODLE   LOOSE

"It's almost time to go home," says Mrs. Jenkins. "But first let's write a story about what we did in school today. Who wants to start?"

"I do!" says Nora. "Today we met Officer Friendly."

"We sang the song 'Old MacDonald Had a Farm,'" says Doris.

"And we built words," say the Franks. "That was fun!"

"Today was a good day," says Timothy. "I can't wait to come back to school tomorrow!"

"Great work, everyone," says Mrs. Jenkins.

You can write a story, too. Get a piece of paper and ask an adult to help you write words to finish these sentences:

My name is . . .

My favorite color is . . .

My favorite food is . . .

Today I went to . . .

I am . . . years old.

Today I feel . . .

 **The Next Step**

Ask an adult to help you write a letter to someone you know. Who do you want to write to? What do you want to say?

Letter to Parents and Educators

The early years are a dynamic and exciting time in a child's life, a time in which children acquire language, explore their environment, and begin to make sense of the world around them. In the preschool and kindergarten years parents and teachers have the joy of nurturing and promoting this continued learning and development. The books in the *Get Set for Kindergarten!* series are designed to help in this wonderful adventure.

The activities in this book were created to be developmentally appropriate and geared toward the interests, needs, and abilities of pre-kindergarten and kindergarten children. After each activity, a suggestion is made for "The Next Step," an extension of the skill being practiced. Some children may be ready to take the next step; others may need more time.

Ready to Read contains activities on elements that support success in beginning reading. The topics covered help children learn to identify the letters and sounds of the alphabet, recognize rhymes, and build simple words. This book also includes components that will help children learn to understand what they read using context clues and sequencing events in a story. Learning to read is a true milestone in a child's life—*Ready to Read* aims to build pre-readers' skills and confidence to prepare them to tackle this exciting challenge.

Throughout the early years, children need to be surrounded by language and learning and love. Those who nurture and educate young children give them a gift of immeasurable value that will sustain them throughout their lives.

John F. Savage, Ed.D.
Educational Consultant